Prop. of
Dan Wakefield

Good Morning

Good Morning

LAST POEMS BY MARK VAN DOREN

Foreword by Richard Howard

Hill and Wang · *New York*

A division of Farrar, Straus and Giroux

"Orbit" was first published by The Pomegranate Press as part
of the American Poets Broadside Series, copyright © 1973 by
Dorothy Van Doren. The following poems have previously ap-
peared in various magazines: "Good Riddance" in *The New
Yorker;* "The Garden of My Own Mind," "And All the While,"
and "The Possessed" in *The Hudson Review;* "Where Have You
Been?," "Pride," "Waking Up," "Human," "The Double,"
"Never Again Shall I," "Death of a Monk (T.M.)," and
"Mountains" in *Art International;* "Apprehension," "Needles
and Pins," "This Has Happened Before," "Water That Falls
and Runs Away," "The Time Has Come," "My Brother Lives
Too Far Away," "The Racehorses," and "The First Poem" in
Voyages, A National Literary Magazine; "Rain Beautifies the
City" and "Water Was" in *The Nation.*

Contents

To Be, While Still Becoming
A Note on the Lyric Verse (1924–72) of Mark Van Doren

In the second half of the twentieth century, we expect—and it is the first half which has whetted, which
has exasperated our expectation—we expect, then, if we
do not quite require, a lyric poem to have the dramatic
impact upon us of suddenness, the convulsive energy of
a pang, and we look in the poem's disposition as we listen
to its discords for that excitement which lurks round the
edges of things, trembling on the verge, thrilling at the
margin. Modernism, as we have come to conceive it in
the century of its life, is not opposed to lyric, but insists
that the implicit qualities of such a poetry be made explicit, demands that the drama inhabiting the simplest
utterance, the slightest acknowledgment of experience
organized above "the tension of the lyre," dwell there in
full view, outrageous, insistent, inescapable. Even at its
most joyous, even when it *celebrates* loss and severance
in an ecstasy, a transport, the modern lyric is committed
to a *tragic role,* a role in which communication with the
divine—and in Western culture such communication
generally takes the disputed form of a protest, a conflict—
is determinant. Love and death, then, in the modern
American lyric are to be excruciating or they are, perhaps, not love and death at all. Only as it approaches
the point of severance from experience is expression con-
sidered severe enough, extreme enough, to be authentic.
This is our modernist heritage, the orthodoxy of a terrible faith in excluded middles; if there is heresy among

us, it has not prevailed—or of course it would no longer be heresy then; heresies are doomed to minority status in poetry, the equivalent of persecution in religion.

But suppose we are confronted with a body, indeed with an anatomy of lyric verse which heretically rejects the tragic immediacy, which prefers to be interesting (the conscious) rather than to be excruciating (the unconscious); which prefers centers to edges, meetings to sunderings; which states—and statement will be a chief tenet of this heretical art:

> *Freedom is the mean of those*
> *Extremes that fence all effort in;*

which chooses—as Mark Van Doren says Shakespeare chose in *The Tempest,* that phantasmagoria of the temporal, as the very title indicates in its root—not so much to tell a story as to fix a vision. Suppose we are to read nearly fifty years' abundance—

> *Leave them all there,*
> *Old lover. Live on*

—of a man's lyric poems (and abundance appears to accompany statement as the idiosyncrasy of the heresy, its necessary condition) and find the drama, or the dramatic, at least, occluded, elided, no more than implicit in the old way. Why then, for us, such a man's poems would be as problematic as, say, Donne's songs and sonnets must have seemed to an admirer of Campion's, a "saying" indeed, when what was listened for was a song; whereas here the expectation is the bright incision that proceeds from the broken speech, the fragmented oracle, and what we are given is the integrity of the fabric, the one vision:

> *To wish a word unsaid,*
> *To wish a deed undone—*
> *Be careful, for the whole*
> *World that was is one.*

Calling a poetry problematic, whether Donne's or Van Doren's, is merely an acceptable, modernist way, of course, of calling it unfashionable. What is meant is that, insofar as we are "modernists," we are troubled by characteristic features of that poetry, in this case by its ease, profusion, recurrent pattern, confidence in the evidence:

> *Eternity is now or not at all:*
> *Waited for, a wisp: remembered, shadows.*
> *Eternity is solid as the sun:*
> *As present; as familiar; as immense.*

I have suggested that two of the characteristic features of this problematical poetry, this heretical lyricism, are the willingness to make statements and the necessity to be prolific; there are others, especially the commitment to that schedule of repetitions and returns we call, significantly, verse. In fact, there would seem to be a tradition or at least a convention for dealing with a world to which the poet refuses to grant our convulsive tragic lineaments, a convention of recurrence, of insistent pattern whereby the world is held in thrall to humble engagements, attentions that come back again, "submissive to each part / till it becomes the all," as Mark Van Doren says.

Now a heresy or a problematics which has its own convention is already a very special kind of heresy—it is more likely to be a discredited but not really lost religion, like matriarchy, which cannot quite be stamped out of our experience because it has somehow, at some level, enabled that experience in the first place, the first time, despite the orthodox practices which would rewrite history in terms of patrimonies, which would *invent* history to replace authentic experience. Enabling in its dealings with duration, its transactions with time (for Van Doren, explicitly, there is always another occasion, a chance to return to the form: "my mind," he exults, "will survive this song," ready and willing to find its further life in yet another song), the lyric poetry which is not singularizing or sundering in its effect, its effort, the "minor" utterance which is profuse and even didactically assertive in its animal integrations—such a poetry probably antedates, certainly underlies our modern orthodoxy of *terribilità* and its searing wisdom of confines, of transgressed limits, for it is the song of

. . . the middle world
That was made as if by children,
Nor is changed with growing old.

We may trace the articulation of such a convention for
dealing with the acknowledged bonds of life which the
Romans called *pietas* and we call religion when we think
of religion as a binding, a *ligament* uniting all experience,
from its most exalted reaches to its meekest resignations
—in our century we may honor this heresy in poems by
Hardy, by Walter de la Mare, by Robert Graves, by
Yeats before 1916, by Robinson and Frost in their lower
registers, and by almost the entire lyric corpus of Mark
Van Doren. The decorum of this kind of poetry admits of
sharp observation but not much experiment or originality
with the tools of that observation, either words or senses.
The language of this poetry, a language invariably acces-
sible to children and to enchantment—to spells and
charms and invocations—is one already received by poets
(all magic depends on repetition), not invented to satisfy
new needs. Hence the many *poetical* words, the archaic
turns, the inversions for the sake of a rhyme, the cunning
topiary of the verses. "What was habit," as Mark Van
Doren says in a poem from this convention of counting,
"now is myth."

Indeed, in one of his very first collected poems, dating
from 1924, appropriately in the form of directions or sig-

nals to a child, initiating the new being into that cycle of expectations which concerns, explicitly, the sense that experience is not single, drastic, separable, but rather recurrent, connective, predictable—experience is versification—in "To a Child with Eyes," Van Doren gives a determinative order for this kind of poetry:

> *Run and see, and say how many.*
> *There are more if there is any.*

Which will be true, and Van Doren true to it, for fifty years: the poet inventories the world ("omission is murder"), loyal to each perception, willing to loiter over each notation, each node on the humming wire which communicates the felt life, confident that all will come round again if only the immediate experience is cherished, embraced, *espoused;* no mere exercise in technical ingenuity, as Theodore Roethke marveled over a poem like "Private Worship," a single metaphor is carried without a break "through thirty lines to a true climax; the theme is not exhausted but enriched by the successful application of the single figure." "There are more" is the faithful corollary of a final prayer, that characteristic vocative of "Mark Van Doren, who grows daily older,"

> *. . . O world*
> *Stay with me till I die.*

Throughout is the trust in accompaniment, the fealty of body to earth, of flesh to spirit, of mind to matter ("my

reason is mortality, and dim / senses"); the religion of
this poetry is an entirely earthly *matter* ("this life of
mine ... lives only here, in this old / building," the poet
says toward the end of his life, resolute to abide by the
given, his faith in appearances never precluding his
fondness for secrets: "Consult the shown, / Believe in the
unshown"). Between that first assertion of plurality and
the last plea for plenitude, there loom—surely the right
word here, a constant weaving of the speech shuttle, as
Sophocles calls it—more than six hundred pages of just
that middle, that central life which is so ruthlessly excluded from the "modern" lyric, that connective tissue,
cartilage, sticking plaster, call it, of a life which is indeed
between—the one life to be found, as the title of Van
Doren's median poem calls it, "Midland":

> *Under the great cold lakes, under the midmost*
> *Parallel that Lisbon too lies under—*
> *Vesuvius and Corinth, Ararat,*
> *Peking and Chosen, yellow and blue seas*
> *Enormous, then the redwoods, then high Denver—*
> *Under the wet midnorth, under cool Canada,*
> *Swings my own West, directionless; the temperate,*
> *The tacit, the untold. There was I born,*
> *There fed upon the dish of dreaming land*
> *That feeds upon itself, forever sunk*
> *From the far rim, from crust and outer taste,*
> *Forever lost and pleased, as circling currents*

Swim to themselves, renumbering Sargasso
Centuries a wind brings round the world.
There am I still, if no thought can escape
To edges from that soft and moving center,
That home, that floating grave of what would fly
Yet did not, my own boyhood, meditating
Unto no end, eternal where I was.

If we are, in what Henry James once called our in-comparable modernity, vexed by characteristic features of a writer's work, as I have begun to limn them here, for example, we have the comfort of knowing that it is precisely such features which, if we yield to them, if we treat them as significance rather than as defect, will turn out to be that writer's *solution* to what we have called his problematics of composition, of utterance. In the case of Mark Van Doren, our difficulties are, then, his ease, the imperturbable grace, the clarity and radiance of an un-dismembered self—rather of an ego that remembers, or as he calls it, "The Middle Creature":

Man is the one most caught
Between not knowing and knowing:
Neither a beast today
Nor archangel tomorrow.

Man has most need of order
Lest he be nothing now;

So builds to the farthest future;
Yet least is lord of the years ...

Our problem, our vexation, in all the smoothness of this resigned *sagesse,* is our sense of the lack of tragic contention; our dilemma is, just so, the denial of extremity. The poetry of Mark Van Doren, so carefully administered by eye and ear and pulse, is not exciting (it is not on the brink, imperiled, jeopardized by its proximity to the void; in these poems, as lion and lamb in the Peaceable Kingdom,

Experience lies down with doom,
That sleeps again, as history uses);

it is merely—merely! the adverb stands for a world of historical reversals, fashions turned inside out—interesting. And as that word itself tells us at its root, to be *interesting* means to be among and in the midst of things, at the center, *mediate.* We are unaccustomed to the enormous modesty of this position, a modesty which amounts to a repudiation; if one writes from the midst of life, then one must accept, as in Scripture, that we are in death. How rare, then, Van Doren's reticence, and how apt:

Time still is to be
When I am not I.
The speech death makes
Is not special for me.

This is not a poetry of compromise—nothing is left out, the awful is not omitted; what marks Van Doren's particular stance is that it is not opposed:

> *Compounded of all tones, including these*
> *Of stricken ground and hideous green seas,*

this music, rather, accommodates the extremities of experience in order to get it all together, as we say now, and to keep it there. Integrity, wholeness, that is never the tragic goal, the pitch of doom which is the reward of struggle, of denial. "Fate," as Van Doren observes, "comes double if we deny." Rather it is the slow guerdon of centrality—"half between is holy ghost"—which this poet is out for, and into, as he makes the odd invocation to the only divinity forever at his elbow, the least glamorous in all the pantheon:

> *Monotony, be thou my god.*
> *Humdrum, lie close and watch me well . . .*
> *Bind me to what I most desire,*
> *No matter how I twist and frown.*
> *The smile you wear as I say this,*
> *Monotony, is all I wish.*

The answer to such a petition is a peril for poetry—for modern poetry, at least. For the poet who "would have each moment's name / be musical, and sound the same," there is the constant temptation of the lithic mode, that inhumanity of earth where a poet can sit

> *. . . among the stones, himself a stone,*
> *Watching an empty heaven till his mind*
> *Passed out of him and poured the silence full.*

Sometimes the requirements of the fully human—the demands of an emotionally saturated life—are arduous;
sometimes the poet falters: "I think I'll sit / till the stones
turn empty. / They don't mind." But to become no more
than immortal is too easy, the trance which sustains the
flesh beyond centuries omits too much for Van Doren,
and his poetry murmurs and rustles on, *past* the stones,
though it notes that "the spirit best remembers being
mute"—passes on to the life which includes but does not
oppose death:

> *Death is our outline, and a stillness seals*
> *Even the living heart that loudest feels.*
> *I am in love with joy, but find it wrapped*
> *In a queer earth, at languages unapt;*
> *With shadows sprinkled over, and no mind*
> *To speak for them and prove they are designed.*
> *I sing of men and shadows, and the light*
> *That none the less shines under them by night.*

As long ago as 1939, such couplets, their ease and sanity,
made it clear that Van Doren was the appropriate heir of
Dryden—a relationship to which I shall return; but what
most caught the attention of Van Doren's (generally ad-
miring) critics was his accommodation of extremes in the

general tenor—one recalls Edmund Wilson and then John Peale Bishop, especially, who marveled at the poet's apparently out-of-the-way concern with such old-fashioned fidelities as family, region, and the enduring of mortality rather than the striving against it. Since the romantic movement, we have been so accustomed to the imagination as a borderer, dwelling in risk and self-loathing upon the contours and verges of experience, that the impulse toward centrality, toward integrity and accommodation rather than alienation and exclusion ("that's me in the middle," Van Doren exclaims, as anyone might on glimpsing himself in a group photograph, and again, apostrophizing the doleful Don and his lumpy Squire, "halfway between them, that will do"— though who else has the choice,

> Who else could be serene at truth's circumference
> When only the known center of it sings?),

the undertaking to unite seems to us an alien, an inadequate account of our situation, unpromising in drama when it is the dramatic conflict which promises to redeem. A life so firmly natural, so happily given over to the leagues and affections of family, of filiation and paternity, of marriage and companionship, of fraternity most of all, and so proudly committed to its own failing body as well—a life unalienated by the kind of demonic aspirations which have created an entire literature of fragmentation and partiality among us—is an exotic indeed, and what is more, a *mild* exotic, the hardest kind to entertain, to appraise, to answer!

It will go easier for us if, as a prolegomenon to any future reading of Mark Van Doren, we trace even for a moment his profoundly acknowledged debt to the English tradition; almost alone among his contemporaries in this country, as John Peale Bishop pointed out, Van Doren shows no trace of French influence. Praising his 1920 study of Dryden (written, then, well before any of the poetry Van Doren includes in his collected work), T. S. Eliot commended Mark Van Doren especially for illustrating "the very wide range of Dryden's work," not just the satire but the achievement in almost every department, every species of poetry. Dryden is not suggestive, Dryden is everywhere explicit; his verse says what he means it to say ("poets are by too much force betray'd," as Dryden himself observed) and not more than that. Yet Eliot was characteristically prophetic to admire Van Doren's breadth of response, for Dryden's is a range paralleled by Van Doren's own—in fiction, in drama, in criticism, and in almost every department, every species of poetry. The summer before he died, I asked Mark Van Doren for a choice—to adorn an anthology I was compiling—of a preferred poem of his own and of a poem from the past with which his own might sustain interesting relations. With a certain asperity, the poet, who had been my teacher and perhaps my only teacher who thought it worth his while to show that he found fools insufferable, chose Dryden's celebrated elegy on Oldham but refused to specify in his own work beyond that preference of fifty years ago for Dryden. In fact, he insisted that his former student select on his own, out of what is not so much an embarrassment as an embodiment of riches, the *Collected and New Poems 1924–1963*, these quiet yet queerly fierce couplets which belong to the sustained middle register of Van Doren's art:

> *Envy the young who have no words at all,*
> *And the old, for they have had them. Now by wall*
> *In sunshine, or by candle at the dance,*
> *Or corner-warm, stillness is circumstance*
> *Conclusive: there they sit, and no one says*
> *They should be heedful of bright sentences.*
> *Their silence, innocent of insult, tries*
> *For how much truth? Who knows? It may be wise*
> *Or sleepy, may be amorous of death*
> *Or heavy with remembrance—the slow breath*
> *Of sluggards at the goal. Who blames them here*
> *For blinking? They are privileged to peer*
> *Past us, past Him, past anyone at all,*
> *And speak no word, those sitters by the wall.*

On the face of it—the face of language heightened beyond mere speech ("if nothing were to be raised above that level," Dryden warns, "the foundation of poetry would be destroyed"), yet beneath any suspicion of mere spellbinding ("a man is not to be cheated into Passion," says Dryden again, "but reasoned into Truth")—on the face of it, this verse appears docile enough, even decorous in diction, a convention, as I have called it, for dealing with what a man means to say. It is a decorum, though, which admits of—which enforces—a terrible knowledge, rather a wisdom to be had only when language is "received," is handed down, and when a poet knows what is in his hands from another's. This kind of poetry, the poetry of a received idiom, is not, as I have said, a matter of experiment (which is merely experience) or even of originality (which is merely a reversion to origins), but of the chastened admission that his language is the poet's fate as well as his fortune, his doom and not merely his discretion. Hence envy of the young who have no words and of the old who have had them: the silence of the old in Van Doren's poem—like Dryden's farewell to a poet his junior by some twenty-two years—is a kind of valedictory to poetry itself, the acknowledgment that utterance is no more than a task, an obligation, that the uncheated passion is all in the silence. Dryden says somewhere, "To invent a probability and to make it wonderful is the most difficult undertaking in the art of Poetry." That is Mark Van Doren's invention in the poem I have quoted here, the invention in speech of the wonderful probability of silence.

I have not intended my appreciation of Mark Van Doren's lyric canon to serve, in particular, as an introduction to the last book of lyrics. In terms of circumstance, these final poems do represent a departure, for they represent The Departure; unlike the many, many other poems of his long life, the vivid, deciduous poems of *Good Morning* are not written in the midst of life, they are written from the acknowledged edge, they are poems everywhere resonant with the prescience and the presence of death. Yet the awareness of a threshold beside him, like Pascal's abyss, does not cause Mark Van Doren to recoil, to withdraw from life. Rather it is as if the very energies and impulses of his being—remembered, imagined, speculated upon, brooded over—were closer to language, to the one embrace he had always mastered, than ever before. There is no program to these moments of almost visionary awareness, these singular last devotions, save one: to come unpropped, undefended to the moment, to the encounter with life itself. That is why the poet can say:

> *This is the first poem. There was none*
> *Before it. Do not misunderstand me. This*
> *Is the first poem ever.*

Exactly: we shall not misunderstand if we realize that *only* when each poem is the first poem can there be a thousand poems. Otherwise, there is only one poem. It is precisely because he acknowledges the primacy of poems —other men's poems, his own poems—that Mark Van Doren can write each new, first one with "an odd secret excitement, a strange need / to be there with words when the heartbeat happened." He is the precious spokesman, mouthpiece and prolocutor of the single life at that moment when it knows itself to sum up the significance of what is more than single, the meaning of what is many.

RICHARD HOWARD

Good Morning

Good Morning

Good morning to the great trees
That bend above this little house;
Good morning to the wind that comes
And goes among the leaves, and sings;
Good morning to the birds, the grass,
Good morning to the bare ground;
Good morning, pond across the way
That must have opened both its eyes;
Good morning, everything that shines
Or doesn't shine; good morning, mole
And worm and nesting mouse—good morning,
Morning to all things that ever
Were and will be, and that are.

Listen to Us, the Leaves Say

Listen to us, the leaves say,
The lazy leaves, not very loud,
Listen to us, listen to us
Up here in the sun, up here in the wind—
Not very strong, but it never stops—
Shut your eyes and listen to us,
Yes, yes, listen to us
Say little or nothing, or maybe a lot,
All of us leaves here talking at once
To ourselves and each other, each other, each other,
All of us leaves up here in the world.

Where Have You Been?

Where have you been? It is cold, it is dark,
And you didn't come home when you said you
    would.
I waited and waited, and went to sleep,
And woke up thinking I heard—it was nothing,
Not even somebody else, or an animal
Passing the door and stopping and sniffing,
No, not even the ghost of the woman
That lived here once without any husband;
Nobody ever came, they say,
To see that poor young lonesome woman.

My Brother Lives Too Far Away

My brother lives too far away
For me to see him when I would;
Which is now; is every day;
Is always, always; so I say
When I remember our boyhood.

So close together, long ago,
And he the one that knew me best;
He the one that loved me so,
Himself was nothing; this I know
Too late for my own love to rest.

It runs to tell him I have learned
At last the secret: he was I.
And still he is, though time has turned
Us back to back, and age has burned
This difference in us till we die.

That Owl

Did you hear that owl
In the middle of the night
In the middle of the woods
In the middle of a dream
I was halfway having—
Did you, dear one?

Tell me if you heard
The other one answer.
That was the awful thing,
That was the reason
I had to wake up then—
Do you believe me?

Tell me if you think
There could have been danger,
Could have been death
If I hadn't cried out—
Did you listen to me, sweet one,
Calling your name?

When everything else is still,
Night itself makes noises.
You wouldn't think it could,
But it can, in the middle of the mind.

As if creation sighed,
Turning in its bed;
As if minutest thinkings
Ran lengthwise, like veins;

As if a sudden stopping;
A jolt; then cracks appeared;
But not as if they sounded,
Save as light breaks;

As if there were a stepping
Like silk upon the stairs;
But not as if it woke you,
So perfect silence is.

Those Great Clouds There

Those great clouds there,
They float like worlds,
Worlds on the way
To another one—where?

But if I knew that
I wouldn't be here,
I wouldn't be watching,
Wouldn't be wondering—

Worlds, worlds
On the way to the other one,
Slow, slow,
So huge, so white—

Wouldn't be wondering
How far it is home,
How big and how high
The whole of it now.

I Had to Be Secret

I hid the peppermint
Under my pillow
In Grandmother's house
At the top of the stairs.

She wouldn't have minded,
But so I did;
I had to be secret,
For who would have known

I was not as I seemed,
I was double of heart,
I was angel and devil
On different days,

And who could have seen
So deep into me
As to say any moment
Which was which?

There Was a Cat That Came

There was a cat that came
One winter to our door.
Every day he came there,
Wild-eyed and thin,
And ate the meat we gave him;
But never walked in.

Never all that winter,
No matter how we coaxed,
Did he as much as promise
That some day he would—
Oh, there were ways he might have
Had he not been afraid

Of something so much older
Than anything we knew,
And wilder, that one day
We said he was a witch.
He listened; and he never
Came again to his dish.

Rain on Leaves

Rain on leaves,
Drip, thrip, thud, thlong,
Is sewing them forever
To the grass, to the ground:
Is stitching, stitching
The edges of a shroud;
And the middle, crisscross,
To make it last long.

Rain next year,
Drip, thrip, thud, thlong,
Will be sewing leaves again
To the grass, to the ground:
Stitching, stitching
The edges of a shroud;
And the middle, crisscross,
To make it last long.

The Smell of Cold

The smell of cold
Deep back somewhere
As if the earth
Were dragon's breath and it was breathed,
Suddenly, on me and on my hands,
Dirty from playing all day long—
Remember, brother, in the pasture grass,
Running and falling?—knuckles
Leathery with stain,
With bruise—remember,
Brother, how we threw the ball
Till too dark to see?—the smell,
Then, of the cold and of our horny
Hands, as if a dragon
Breathed—on you, too,
Brother. Was it not
So? Remember?

Merry-Go-Round

Horses in front of me,
Horses behind,
But mine is the best one,
He never looks down.
He rises and falls
As if there were waves,
But he never goes under,
Oh, music, oh, mine.

He is steady and strong,
And he knows I am here,
He says he is glad
That I picked him to ride.
But he hasn't a name.
I told him my own,
And he only went faster,
Oh, music, oh, mine.

Around and around,
And the people out there
Don't notice how happy
I am, I am.
The others are too,
But I am the most,
The most, the most,
Oh, music, oh, mine.

Walking in the Rain

Walking in the rain
By myself all alone,
Without anybody here
To notice where I go,
Without any worry
Over when to start home,

Walking in the rain
With the cool coming at me
Like an old friend, softly,
Like—maybe—a lover
Whispering to me, "Hush,
Be still, breathe deep,"

Walking in the rain
By myself all alone
Is having all the warm world
Secretly inside me
All the cool while,
All, all the wet way.

Where I saw the snake
Is where I sometimes go
In deep dreams, desiring
To see his length again
Like the sun's blackness, coiled,
Like the sun's center, pulsing,
With white fire all around.

There was no fire, though.
Only intensest black—
Blue black—not burning,
Yet what do I see now?
The body of him departing
Even as he remained:
Motionless, yet gone,

Leaving a lake of light
On the dead grass; and that
Is where I sometimes go
In deep dreams, desiring
To see him coil again,
Then straightway be elsewhere—
Not anywhere—no.

The Stick, the Stone

Lying on my back, that hurts
From a stick and a stone I didn't see
When I picked this place—but it isn't much,
And I won't move—I study the arching
Branches above me, way up there
Where birch looks like elm, and ash
Fills all the spaces in between,
So sunlight, striking down and in,
Shatters at last to tiny stars,
Diamonds on dark green,
Pinholes in the dome of sky
That isn't sky, but a lace of leaves
And delicate limbs: cloth of the forest,
Woven for me I think this day,
Though certainly it wasn't; no,
A sacred ceiling, not to be looked at
Standing; so I lie and don't
Move; nor do the stick, the stone.

Forgetting and Remembering

As when in shadowy
Water that sometimes the sun
Strikes through, and sometimes not,
And great fish rise up
Or fail to rise—the turtle there
That comes and goes, himself a slow
Shadow—and pebbles on the bottom shine
Circular, like money, shine
Then vanish as the water
Clouds, or if a wind brings ripples—so
Things are, or they are not:
Our own to hold or lose, as never
Intellect, alas,
Nor will, nor wish,
Decides.

Shame

Comes in like a tide
At the wrong time: waves
Of unwelcome warmth flooding
Inmost defenses, parts
Hitherto innocent of wondering whether
Anybody sees; now
Everybody, now
Animals even, winds and weathers,
Worms, flies; now
All created things, each
With its secret pride, wondering whether
You too have it; no,
Not now, not
Ever again, maybe.

The stiffening beneath
The skin, the impalpable armor
We hardly know we have
Till a word pierces it, a look
Undresses, flays us—oh,
Oh, the discovery then
Of who, of what, we all of the time
Were. And still
Are. But must pretend
We still don't know;
Are nothing. Not till then
Does healing happen, do
The torn places close, twice over
Mended, never again
To weaken. So secret,
So impregnable, pride
Is, beneath the skin.

Courage

Courage is knowing more
Than chance does, or fate—
Necessity, even, hung
Like a vulture in heavy air—
Is knowing that these are there
As they cannot know it themselves,
So clumsily they wait
For the unseen moment to strike
Even courage does not know when;
But courage is not surprised
By things outside of its ken
It was taught to anticipate.

Rain beautifies the city;
Makes mirrors of it, flattering
Our minds, our eyes; even
The sparrows, resting, glance at themselves
In windows and think they are cleaner
For once; while cornices drip
And gutters gurgle, and tires
Hiss incessantly, saying
Look, it is different now, listen
And look, it is not the same
City at all, it is old, old—an old
Woman with bright eyes, remembering
The youth of the world, the cool,
The dancing feet, the flung capes, the morning
Cries, the sun, the whistles, and the unkillable
Hope, the unstoppable joy.

Vermont

Perfection in grass,
Grace on the tops of mountains: green
All over, green to the root. The long slopes
Wear darkest green for mourning; green
Is the color of their true love,
Death; green the beginning and the end
Of earth; but no end yet, for time
Goes on almost forever, says
The coolness, says the clearness, says
The sadness; so not yet.

Waking Up

Waking up is being born
All over, as if the first time
Had not been half enough, had been—
Ridiculous—a kind of death.

No, not that, except no light
Broke, no sound was heard, nothing
Moved in the memory, nothing was like
This latter dawn, this daily wonder.

The window there, waiting; the curtain
Lifting a little; the ache in the bones
Already going; yet some of it lingers
In the deep warmness, the delicious

Body of bed. Waking up
Is being born twice over and knowing
That this is so; as if the first
Hour of all were alive again.

Ferns in a Ring

In the middle of May,
In the middle of the meadow,
In the middle of—look,
They are here again.

They have risen in a ring,
They are standing there—see,
It is perfectly round,
The circle they make.

Each beyond the other,
Evenly apart,
They almost move,
Yet the circle is still.

Ferns in a ring,
Just so, just so:
It is how the new universe
Holds its breath.

Descending Water

Once more the music—
Heard, beheld—of leaping
Streams, as down the mountain
Snow water comes, mixed
On March days with blowing
Rain, so that the heard,
Seen music sounds
And looks like all creation
Delivering this day
Its secret, even in level
Pools where, passionate,
Black water hesitates,
Barely breathing, then
Plunges—even
There.

Leaving Valentines

In those days
We feared one another:
Boy, girl,
We both were humble,
Wondering how
We could ever be worthy
Of words that were loving,
Of eyes adance.

In those days,
In that town,
We rang the bell
And sprinted away;
But watched in darkness
The opening door
And the lifting up
Of what we had left.

What we had left
Was a piece of ourselves.
The lacy paper
With hearts upon it
Burned to be taken
For true, for true—
The words unspeakable:
Who loves who?

I Hear the House Is Gone

I hear the house is gone
Where two old people slept
And woke and slept again—
Forever, I thought then.

Oh, I was wrong. Change
Makes every person strange;
A grandchild, even—
Himself is not the same;

Thinks only now and then
Of those two there;
No wonder they departed
And took their house to where

Memory is faithful,
And sound never fades:
The old man yawning;
Her deep silences;

These, and the very windows,
With ferns in them; the door;
The plum trees all around,
And the high elms before.

A Dream of Trains

As long ago they raced,
Last night they raced again;
I heard them inside me,
I felt the roll of the land.

I looked out of a window
And I was moving too;
The moon above Nebraska,
Lonely and cold,

Mourned for all of the autumns
I had forgotten this:
The low hills that tilted,
The barrenness, the vast.

I think I will remember now
Until the end of the world
How lordly were the straightaways,
How lyrical the curves.

Gypsies

I think I don't remember—
Or do I?—how their eyes
Were deeper in and darker
Than any ever known.

It was a famous day
They passed my father's gate,
With horses fore and after,
And women walking slow—

I think I've only heard
Of how their waists were small,
And how the skirts they moved in
Mysteriously whirled.

But then I seem to see this
As if it were again;
I even hear the bridles,
The bracelets, and the sound

Of someone humming weirdly
Inside the caravan.
It must be I was there then.
Or was I, alas?

Needles and Pins

Black was the color of the peddler's wagon,
And black the doors inside the door
He opened, talking: little doors
On silver hinges, double doors
No bigger than his hand, that waited,
Waited till my mother said,
"And what is that in there?" "Oh,"
Said he, "needles." "But I've got
Needles." "Not like these. Or pins—
Look—with ruby heads. And as
For thimbles—try those on, they fit
Like second fingers." "What's in this one?"
"Scissors, madam—English." "What's
In here?" "The perfect thread." "Aha!"
"Don't laugh. Unbreakable." "I don't
Believe it. Dress goods?" "Why, of course.
With patterns out of Paris." "Pooh!"
"Fancy combs, or plain. Mirrors,
Madam—boxes for your jewelry—"
"Have none." "Don't believe it—here!"
A glass necklace. "No"—shaking
Her head as the tired horse shook his;
And the little doors clicked, and the big one closed,
And off went Rumpelstiltskin, mumbling.

Nobody then knew where we were,
From four to six nobody knew.
Nor do I now, nor do I need to;
What I remember is not a place.

Nor a time. So what do I remember?
Something so new it had no name,
Something so old it needed none.
It was being out, it was running free

Down Oregon Street past home, past neighbors,
Then disappearing from sound, from sight,
From anyone's caring, for no one called.
We were out of the world till dusk and supper.

And where we were was everywhere,
Or it might have been, so sweet and free
Was the feel of it in November's air—
Or April's—and the smell of it.

These Drops of Rain That Hang

These drops of rain that hang and don't
Fall, beads on the delicate black
Branch, the horizontal one
There by the window, temporary
Splendor for no eye but mine:
In another hour the sun that makes them
Brilliant now will quietly
Remove them—goodbye, diamonds—still,
Sweet is the glistening, like lady's
Tears that lie and are not wiped
Away—not yet—delicious tears—
Sweet is the wealth that came to me
Not even for my asking, sweet
Drops of rain that hang, that hang.

The Buchanan Graves

Slowly, slowly up the green
Hill, and then we looked down:
Not at all the world, though;
Only at a pair of names,

Only at two silences
That joined the others, close and far.
The whole hill was one great
Hush that hovered his and hers,

That took them in and let them be;
That even listened, as death does
To muteness singing one more note,
And makes no music in reply.

Human

Nothing in all the world,
Not even the great globe,
Compares unto mercy,
Or longed-for love.

Or for that matter hate:
Cruelty's hoarse throat;
Anything that measures,
So deep, the heart.

Nothing is at all—
Buildings, the sea—
Without joy for witness,
Or misery.

"I'm not afraid."
"No? Why did you jump then?"
"That was just a goose walking
Over my grave."

"Silly old saying."
"Yes, but I shivered
For no earthly reason—or
Was there, I wonder?"

"Was what?" "A reason.
Where *is* my grave?
And who else is in it?" "Now!
Who's not afraid?"

Time Was a Single Rose's Death

Time was a single rose's death
Seemed ample subject for a song,
And she who sang it wept with me
For life so short, for love so long.

Sweet woe. But now—oh, end of time—
No tears, no music. Who can sing
Of roses gone when men predict
Some day the death of everything?

Time was I thought if one thing went,
Or two, or more, the rest remained.
The singing was for that—oh, lovely
While before the prophets reigned.

Sing a new song
With yet an old burden.
Ancient of days,
Sing a new song.

Sing a new song
Of how it was always,
How it still is,
And how it must be.

Sing a new song
Of gladness and sadness,
Each of them older
Than music or word.

Sing a new song
Like the old, the old ones.
Ancient of days,
Sing a new song.

Grandparents' Houses

They must have magnets in them, set
For certain persons only: set
For these that come—hear the high
Voices—suddenly in summer
Up the leafy road, exclaiming
Who knows what till they arrive
In silence at the door—surprise,
Surprise—then in, familiarly,
As if they knew the smell of the rooms,
As if they now were where the pull
Of dark invisible iron had brought them:
Children once removed, magic
Offspring with the eyes of others,
Most at home here of all places.

The Way a Mouse Runs Up a Wall

The way a mouse runs up a wall
If it's rough enough and she's frightened enough
Is the way you can have a thought then lose it—
What was it, when did it go, where is it
Now? It's gone for good, too, isn't it? No?
Then why that look, as if you were listening
To four small feet overhead somewhere
In the highest house there ever was,
Not yours, oh, no, not anybody's
With a name that still can be remembered.

The Double

Where shall I find that other one
Whose double you are, or so I dreamed?
Why should I look, if I have you?
Why should I think of her at all?

I must, though. It is very strange
Even in sleep to have seen you there
When of course you were here by my own side.
Should I be telling you this? I wonder.

Don't look away. The other one stared
Straight at me for the longest time.
And then the sweet, the sober smile
As if you saw me in a mirror.

But I saw you. What am I saying?
Don't laugh. I grant, it is very strange.
Two of you and one of me.
If even me. If undiminished.

Everything Went Still

Everything went still.
I had the power, and used it.
Never in all of time
Had there been such quiet.

I shouted my own name;
Listened, and held my breath.
But it didn't come back to me.
Echo itself was deaf.

So I said, let there be sound.
But the silence did not cease.
Until I woke—oh, then,
The ringing in these ears.

Oldest Miracle

That there should be a brain—
That body should move itself—
Must have been such a dream
As madmen say they have.

The Time Has Come

And when he came he spoke with the hoarsest
Voice anyone here had ever
Heard, saying "The time has come,
The time has come. Nobody now
Can be prepared. Too late, too late."

"What time has come?" He looked at us
With pity so deep, we already
Wept. "You know." And so we did.
All of those others we hadn't believed,
But him we did. And why was that?

For still nothing has happened. And yet
We know it will. What will? He didn't
Say; he turned and went. But the sound
In his throat was enough: as if the bottommost
Boards of the world were tearing loose.

Apprehension

As birds on the lawn, busily feeding,
All of a sudden are off—
What could have scared them? None of us knows,
None even of them perhaps, yet surely
Something, if only a whiff,
A whisper of possible death—
Off together, like so many arrows, off
And up and into the trees—
Ah, if only our imminent end
Could announce itself so neatly; if only
Contagion in us were as swift as that.
And as soon forgotten; for one at a time
They drop back down and begin again.
Ah, the forgetting. If only that.

Sweet Sleep

Let it come in by the door, by the window,
Let it find out some crack in the wall,
Let it be here all at once, from nowhere,
Let it be like nothing else in the world.

Nothing is like it because it is nothing;
Not even softness—oh, beyond that;
Not even something that has to be nameless;
Not even going and not coming back.

Sleep is a melting away, a sweetness
That swims into view then is gone, is gone,
As if air were ocean, and things in it sank
Out of touch, out of taste, as day became night.

We Find It Hard to Bear

We find it hard to bear, the slow,
The certain death of things: all things
At last, but these things now; as when
The bird no longer comes and sings
That used to wake us in the half
Dark; and then we slept again,
Smiling. Where now is that little
Throat, and where in all of morning's
Glory is the echo of that thin
Extravagant music, much too big
For where it came from? So we said,
Not meaning it, for song so brave,
So full has never again been heard
By the opening flowers, by the listening sky.

How Praise a World That Will Not Be

How praise a world that will not be
Forever? Stillness then. Time
Sleeping, never to wake. No prince's
Kiss. No prince. Praise? Even
The echo of it dies, even
Memory, in the last brain
That loved it, withers away, and mind
Not even dozes, being done
With work that mattered not at all.
How then praise nothing?
                        Yet that day
Has never dawned. Here is the world
So beautiful, being old, so
Mindful of its maker—what
Of him when that day comes—you say
It must—what then of him, and of this
Place so crowded with his creatures—
With us all—oh, praise the time
That's left, praise here and now, praise
Him that by his own sweet will
May suddenly remake the world
Forever, ever, ever, ever.

This Ground So Bare

This ground so bare, so beaten by winter,
Suddenly sends up delicate green,
Then blue, then yellow and red, then white:
Secrets it was saving for us,
Wealth we didn't know we had.

Who could believe in weary March
That the dun slope, the bitten meadow,
And here by the house, border and bed
Would ever again be what they could be:
Flame, flame, wonderful, wordless—

Oh, but their stillness, the standing plants,
Oh, but their coolness, the burning blossoms,
Oh, but the miracle from nowhere,
Light out of darkness, gold out of poverty,
Blessing beyond any thinkable dream.

Marsh Marigolds

Marsh marigolds at the water's edge,
Stay with me longer, let your feet
Be cool and wet forever, cowslips
(Do you like your old name better?
Never mind, you know who's talking),
Cowslips with so many yellow
Faces, all rejoicing there
In light yourselves created—air
And water, sun and mirror, gold
Somehow resulting—stay with me
At least a little longer, now
That May elsewhere is dying, cowslips,
Cowslips that must go to sleep
With summer—yes, I know, but please
Not yet awhile, bright marigolds.

Water That Falls and Runs Away

Water that falls and runs away,
You are my friend, you talk to me.

Where you come from, where you go,
You never tell me, though I know.

What are you saying then all day,
Over and down and away and away?

For I do listen, my sweet friend,
And will until the world's end;

Nor do I beg you to declare
More than sky does, more than air,

Where you come from, where you go,
Which I only dream I know.

Farewell, My Little

Farewell, my little no one,
Farewell, my small nobody,
Farewell, my next to nothing,
Farewell, my nit, my sweetest
Perfection of non-being.

But I'm not really going,
Not leaving you, my tiny,
My particle, my atom,
Not losing you, my diamond
That lights the world at last.

Never Again Shall I

Never again shall I,
Never again shall we—
Look—that cloud—how huge,
How high can beauty be?

There was no room in the world
For this great thing that is there.
Yet look—it even increases.
Whiteness is everywhere.

Dusk at the edges, though,
Then softness so deep within,
Beauty itself is sleeping
Till Doomsday shall have been.

This Life of Mine

This life of mine, so secret even
To me that when I fish the black
Water I startle turtles, and bring up
Blind trout, and more too
That I won't tell you of because
I don't know the names—not yet
I don't, but soon I will because
I must—this life of mine, so wild
In its surprises, bitter and sweet
By turn, hideous, lovely, cruel,
Kind, lives only here, in this old
Building, where if I come it lets me
In, and what we say to each other
Then—why, that's nobody else's
Business; even the water snake
Sinks and rises for its own
Reasons, which I never know.

Wind Is Not Modest

Wind is not modest, it lets us
Know it is there, it masters
All languages, uses
Every thing that's loose:
Leaves, milkweed silk,
Vain butterflies, small
Birds that go like sparks,
Like seeds sailing; smoke,
Bullied as it tries to rise
Then sent off tattered, tumbling;
Snow, everywhichway
Whitening the whole
World; rain driving
Grey waterfalls before it;
Sleet, seaside sand
Cutting our faces; clouds
On a blue day, majestically
Moving; waves far out,
Close in—no matter—
Mounting each other; dust,
Suddenly up and off,
Restless, whirling sometimes
Briefly in dance, though sometimes
The strength behind it grows
Terrible, uprooting
Oaks, scattering the boards
Of houses, levelling all
There ever was of a certain

Town—blast of tornado,
Hurricane, and tidal
Death along the coast;
But then, too, the gentlest
Kiss on cheeks, on eyes,
From the soft South; and sounds
Borne, of bells, of voices,
Of dogs barking, as clothes
On a line flap, and treetops
Bend a little, studying
How not to break when the roar
Comes—see, says the wind,
I'm here; listen, feel,
Look—oh, all of these,
Then more; forever here.

The Racehorses

I can remember them back there
In time so old and far away
It must have been somebody else
They breathed upon. And yet not so,
For still I hear them, and my mind
Cannot forget those frantic feet,
Those blowing nostrils, and the foam
That flecked their shoulders as they passed.

For they did overtake me then.
Not now. They are not there at all.
But I can remember how they raced
Unevenly, breaking their several
Hearts to come abreast of each other
Then on for my mind to follow—on,
On—oh, when did the sound of their going
Cease? And what did it sing, did it say?

The First Poem

This is the first poem. There was none
Before it. Do not misunderstand me. This
Is the first poem ever. No hint,
No help, no host of cousin, uncle, father
Objects, no mother language, nothing to start from
Except the silence, nothing to run with save
An odd, secret excitement, a strange need
To be there with words when the heartbeat
   happened,
When the walls of the world, listening to each other,
Sighed, and I caught the sense of it
And fitted it to sound, as afterward
I did again when the great walls, groaning,
Grew louder; yet not deafening; the wonder
Even then was the clearness, was the joy.

Water Was

What did the first man
Think water was?
So thin, so dripping, so
Weightless between the fingers, so
Perfectly seen through, with fish gliding
As if in captured air, and ripples
Kissing the top of it, where wind and wave
Argued which was lighter. Then,
Neither was: the two together, monstrous,
Walls of weight that crushed all thought
Of breathing. Then,
Quiet once more, then nothingness—
Transparency—till one day a vessel
Filled, and backs bent
To lift it: vainly, for the invisible
Contents were bound as if by iron
To earth: heavy, not
Gamesome, so that— look, a little lake
Must lie there like lead, and seven solid
Oceans outweigh the world.

Jungle

The trunks so old and tall,
And the canopy so dense:
What does sunlight do,
Aching to get in?

The vines so serpent strong,
Disappearing in one another:
How far is it to where
Green leaves wave in wind?

The silence like an anthem,
And then the screams of birds:
When is the morning over,
And how does night come?

The forest floor so clean—
Beware of scorpions, though—
A man might run a mile
On nothing more than moss.

A man might lay him down
And never get up again,
Here in these halls of dawn,
This paradise of dusk.

Those Children There

Those children there
On the hayload going home
To supper: seven round heads,
All shining—not a one of them was dark
To begin with, nor has changed, all silver
Still, all thistledown; as light, too,
Where they sail serenely through the late day,
Scarcely moving on their bales, but talking,
Yes, I hear them, and waving to me
As they pass: these worker bees,
These helpers of their father, who will never
Thank them when they come, the eldest driving,
The youngest needing to be lifted down—
Never thank them any more than bees
Thank one another, coming, going,
Necessary, busy in the sun.

She Does Not Know

She does not know how many
Eyes are upon her here.
Old eyes. All of them
In this room adore her.

Nor do they wish it known,
Even to themselves.
No, let her believe her mother
Is the only one that cares:

Her mother there, who watches
The beauty showing through;
Yet is afraid, as the child is,
Of what may happen then;

And as these ancient minds are
That keep the secret safe:
The modesty of maidens
Is not to be surprised.

Let her believe that someone—
Ah, but her lips are burning
With syllables a stranger
Will have to be answered with:

The young one who is coming
Through hemispheres of dark;
The sweet one who is feeling
Already where she is.

Rapunzel, Rapunzel

Rapunzel, Rapunzel,
Let down your golden hair
As far as to the top step
Of the stone stair,

The stone stair, Rapunzel,
That goes on down forever.
There is no coming up again,
Ever, ever, ever.

Rapunzel, Rapunzel,
Nevertheless I came.
For love of you I climbed it.
Here then I am.

Rapunzel, Rapunzel,
Be kind to me at last.
Let down your long and golden hair—
But haste, Rapunzel, haste!

Vertigo

Instead of the world turning,
I turn the world: walls,
Ceilings, and then outdoors
Whole trees, whole banks of cloud—
Be wary of me, world,
My strength is terrible.

Except that it is weakness,
Too. This shouldn't be.
My head, my heart: all hollow.
And no legs—Lord,
No legs. How then can I
Turn anything? And so

I shut my eyes. But round,
Around it goes, and can't
Be stopped. No question now
Where the power is. Not in me.
In the world. I'm nothing—less
Than nothing—to great That.

Good Riddance

I threw him as far as Thor
Would have thrown his hammer if Thor
Had been here, but Thor wasn't;
He slept in deepest eternity,
As I did not. I woke,
And it was a dream. So now
There was still in the world this hideous
Soul—if soul—that I would never
Again in all of time
Be able to cast out.
As if I had the right?
Ah, but in dream I did,
And the will, too, and the might.
I was almost Thor, was almost
Thunder; but not quite.

The Garden of My Own Mind

The garden of my own mind—
Who tends it, for it isn't me?
Who changes it by night, by day?
Who kills it then who gives it life:
Newborn color, and strength again?

Every flower in it can die—
Has died. And been by whom replaced?
I wish I knew; I'd worship death
Could I be told his other name:
The one that brings the freshness in,

The one that helps me to forget
Whatever died, as all things do
Except these now that are my own,
Except these blossoms that I breathe,
Except all this that is my life.

And All the While

And all the while,
Down under,
Something lives
That I can't see,
Though it is mine,
Though it is me.

Without me here
It wouldn't be there;
But neither could I
Be more than I am—
Which is what I desire—
Were I wholly alone.

I must not try
Too hard or too long,
Or even at all,
To guess what it is:
So ancient, so still,
So known and unknown.

This Has Happened Before

I am not alone.
This has happened before.
Tell me, Time,
How often and where—

How far back,
And who were the ones?
Too many, I know,
And faint are the names.

Faint are the breaths
And the fingerprints
Of all those companions
So long since gone,

So nowhere now
Except that they press
And listen and feel
The invisible glass:

Memory's moths,
Of whom I am one,
Practicing here
For oblivion.

The Possessed

The strength in me is not mine.
Not anybody's. It is too much
For one heart to hold, for one
Mind to make welcome here
In the world where strength is a strange thing—
Listen. This is not me talking,
Not even the wind, not even waves
Breaking. What you hear and see
Is the truth coming through, the iron
Entering, then lingering, then
Leaving on its terrible errand
To others, who will know it is not
Their own, it is so strong, so strange,
So cruel; and beautiful past bearing.

The time for it, I think,
Is marked upon the wall
Between my mind and yours—
Oh, but there is one,
Of air and isinglass,
And it is made to fall
As time is made to pass.

Time and tea together
Are such a magic thing
As emperors once dreamed of;
And empresses, left lonely
At darkening of day,
Clapped hands as if to frighten
The woe of the world away.

Truelove

"Father, what is truelove,
That they sing about?"
"It's something, little daughter,
You can do without."

"Mother, what is truelove?
I'm old enough to know."
"If you were, my darling,
I would tell you so."

"Brother, what is truelove?
Be serious with me."
"I will. But it is something
That cannot ever be."

"Sister, what is truelove?—
Oh, dear, why are you crying?"
"Because someone has left me,
And my heart is dying."

Rachel Weeping for Her Children

Rachel weeping for her children,
Ceres searching through the world,
Eurydice down under there—
How is it that I hear sometimes
Their broken voices blended so
That pain in them seems pure and one?

In dream it is the sweetest sound,
However far it has to come,
However ancient the dark air
It pierces, lighting its own way;
In dream the wildest sorrow sings
As if there were no sorrow yet,

As if there were no death in the world,
As if no daughter had been lost,
As if no lover looked behind.
(O woe that will not be forgot,
O longing still unsatisfied,
Forgive us. We remember you.)

So Big a Thing

Why am I so serious today,
My only love? You ask, and I cannot exactly
Say; except that somewhere,
So far away
I'm tired with trying to imagine
That much distance, that much air
And land—
Time, too—
Listen.
Somewhere, so long ago
Who now would know,
A thought started coming,
Coming, and at last is here,
Is here; but is so big a thing, so like a moving
Cloud, yet, oh, so slowly
Moving, like a world
Of weather with great storms in it
That do not break, that do not strike—
My only love, it cannot be
That this huge weightless thing
Was meant for me,
This thought that isn't in words
And never will be, yet it started
Coming, coming, and at last
Is here.

Old Man, Old Woman

Old man, if he cares much
When old woman is achesome, gives
No sign to strangers; even when
She staggers, seems not to notice

But does, and old woman knows it
In the odd way of animals
That watch each other incessantly.
Such tenderness is in these two,

Each of them sees everything
Outside, inside the other: old
Man, old woman suffer and then
Feel good together, their hearts equal,

Their eyes veteran, missing no
Least message, morning or evening,
Winter or summer, during or after
Pain—oh, dear, plenty of that.

Death of a Monk
(T.M.)

The best bottle of the best wine
Tipped over all at once and spilled—
Catch it, save it, but nobody
Could. Nothing left but the fragrance.

Which remains. Miraculous,
It fills all air, and is sweeter daily;
And sharper, for this merry mind
Had knives in it, had indignation.

Which could not kill the kindness, did not
Dim the holy brightness—or
We thought it holy; otherwise
How came his wit was never weary?

My Friend's Daughter

Kinship so fine,
If any at all—
But yes, it is gold
Hair split, it is gossamer
Lengthwise divided—

Something that binds
This daughter to me—
And yet no daughter,
And yet no binding,
For she is free—

Sometimes I wonder
What the name of it is:
This silken relation,
This love that is less,
That is more, than I know.

Hospital: Midnight

Each in his cave, medicined
For sleep, yet studious of sound
And ceiling: every angle there
Eloquent of something thought
But sooner forgotten than it was said.
No matter, though. The silence here—
Footsteps in the hall, but going
Elsewhere—now they're gone—good—
The silence, silence. Centuries
Of silence in a nutshell—room
406—remember? Yes.
Turn over now. Then back again.
Who groaned? Footsteps in the hall—
Count them—that will tell me who—
Count them, count them—that will tell—

Lady She Was

Good name, good dog:
Lady she was,
Perfect in worship,
Queen of quiet.

Could run with the deer,
But then came home.
Except this once.
What huntsman shot her?

Would he believe
There could be such sorrow?
Only an animal?
Let him listen.

Two-Minded

They beg to be left alone;
Then when they are, what riot—
Unheard, though—in the atoms
That certify their souls.

To be, and not to be noticed:
There is no mind can endure
The thought of such death forever.
So the molecules start dancing,

Secretly, in anger
At us who have turned away;
In hope, though, of our witness
Before their time to die.

Mountains

So movingly they show themselves—
Rise away, worlds on end,
And mystify our minds that watch
Yet never see the same shape twice,
As if they dreamed, as if they breathed,

As if—oh, what to say of those
Great things that have no voices, have
No eyes, and yet they live, they show
Their shoulders; have no heads, and yet
Somewhere within them time remembers.

The silence of it takes my breath,
Considering, believing; blinds
My eyes, that cannot hope to see
Six hundred million miles ahead
To where I'll be twelve months from now—
Here, only here, but oh, meanwhile
The necessary swiftness of it
Dizzies me; the smoothness, too,
As of a perfect engine rounding
Curve on curve then straight away
As if forever; yet not so,
For the swinging is incessant—soft
The turning, light the going, slow
The moving after all, if seen
From nowhere: thistledown, suspended,
Floating, come to rest in my
Own mind that cannot feel or hear
The wind—there is no wind—O endless
World out there, O emptiness,
Receive the roundness that I ride on,
Save it, save it, as you save
The sun its master, save the circling,
Let the speed of it not falter,
Let the swiftness not diminish,
Though the terror of it slay me.

Master Dog

With fox feet and upright ears
He trots beside me or lopes ahead
And waits—I am slow—then is with me again
Till the next excitement. Yet nothing compares
With Him, there, I think he is saying,
Nothing, nobody, here or at home;
His very slowness, I think he is saying,
Means more than all the run of the world.
While I am thinking how I do envy
The spring in his ankles, the hope in his eyes,
The speed of his going and then his returning,
The grace of his lying down. I am his
Exactly as he is mine, I am saying,
And he does not hear it, the humble one.

Singing

The sound of it so changes me,
I wonder who I ever was.
Where did I live until this time
When suddenly—but how to say
What happens when the singing starts?

The sound of it so magics me,
I'm no more in this world at all.
The glory and the power of it,
The kingdom and the sweetness—joy,
Joy that such a thing can be,

That voices can surpass themselves
And angels take the place of men;
That human throats—oh, high, oh, low,
Oh, passionate beyond compare—
Make heaven's music perfect here.

Sadness

Sadness wants no company,
It loves to be alone, and is,
Whether or no; in thickest throngs
It feeds upon its dark-eyed self
As beauty does, as melancholy.

Sadness is the sweet queen
Of a small country with no subjects
In it. Sadness is the face
All men, all women wear when only
God, they think, is there to see them.

Sudden, or not at all.
Like light, like air, a finest
Nothing. Comes unplanned
And goes forgotten—please,
Please, forgotten, as pain
Can be, as pleasure. Tears
And smiling mixed, like motes
In sunbeams, unexpected
Sparks from a spent log—
Sudden, then midnight there.

Strength

Terrible unweighed,
Unmeasured. Terrible
Enough known; yet better
Known; for until then, more
Than mind can imagine, more
Than nightmare invent. Strength
For that matter is sometimes gentle—
The giant was kind—yet only
Sometimes. Now? Who knows?
To be feared or not to be feared—
Which is it? Philosopher,
Teach us how to decide.

What If I Still Could Run

What if I still could run,
What if I still could play,
Having no thought of tomorrow
Because it was not today?

What if I still were lightfoot,
What if I still were strong,
What if all afternoons
Of my life were endless long?

For that is how I remember—
Oh, time that never passed—
Eternity's rehearsal
Before black night at last.

Red Squirrel

Quick, quick, the tree,
Then up, then up—oh, no?
Down suddenly, then off?
Well, you know best—or do you?
Kinsmen have been caught,
The cat's quick too—look there,
He's coming. Up again!
And Little Red, stay hidden.
You'd love to see, I know,
We all know; but keep
For God's sake out of sight
This once—for my sake, say.
The other side of the trunk—
That's right—now stay there,
Stay there. Unless of course
You have to prove your kind
Is curious, have to prove
All over again what all of us
Know—it's even in books—
Have to make plain what kills you,
Kills you. No life else?
Well, you know best. Or do you,
Do you? I give up.

In the Time Left

In the time left,
With the strength given,
What can be done
That is worthy of heaven?

If anything is,
And if anyone merits,
So far down here,
The attention of spirits.

But if someone does,
What then shall he do?
What shall he dream of
All the night through?

Ah, that's enough.
Dreaming suffices:
Offspring of time
With eternity's faces.

Nothing but Plants

These great old trees—strange, strange—
Are nothing but plants that have been here forever.
Not quite forever, either; once
They were delicate, might not have lived,
Had silken stems that could bend to the ground,
Were tenderly green, drank dew in the night;
And still—strange—are nothing but plants,
However enormous, however high,
However like rock to lean on; fixed
Deep in earth; rough to the touch
Like those old men there—what were those old
    ones—
Strange, strange, what were they once?

Thanksgiving Day

Hours without edges flow together
As the long afternoon, somnolent, keeps
Poor watch on the passing of time, that has
No shape any more, and small ambition.

Today melts back into yesterday,
And tomorrow will never arrive, say these
Who came to be with us, and now so sleepily
Go, with kisses drifting between us

And goodbyes, sweet on the autumn air,
Being our benediction. So
May dark come down and the day end,
Say we; this day that is like no other.

What Now, What Next

What now, what next,
What never at all,
For time is flying
Faster than I am,
And something today
Is nothing tomorrow,
Tomorrow, tomorrow,
If such there be.

What the day after,
Sons of the morning,
Daughters of moonlight,
What the next hour,
What next if any,
Eyes of this evening,
Watching and waiting
So serious there.

Meteorology

Great whirling weathers,
How come you so fast,
How come you so far?

Great wheels of wind,
Who sees you, O ruthless
Right arms of the Lord?

Overnight you arrive,
Great spinners of chaos
As old as the world.

And yet no chaos—
O great whirling weathers,
How come you so true?

Out of This Window

Out of this window
Is half the world:
A whale's eye,
Small and enormous.

The west half.
Rumors of sunrise
Only: long
Shadows. That shorten,

Then the high sky.
Then lengthen, preparing
For sunset. Afterward,
Stars. I see them all down.

By Mark Van Doren